KINDERGARTEN
SUMMER WORKBOOK
BEAUTY IN BOOKS

This Book Belongs to:

Name _____   Date _____

SUMMER VOCABULARY

Identify the pictures below. Use the word bank below to name each picture.

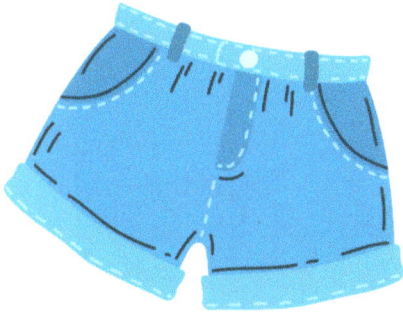

_____
....
_____

_____
....
_____

_____
....
_____

_____
....
_____

Word Bank:

shorts	dress	bikini	flip flops

Name ———————————— Date ————————————

SUMMER VOCABULARY

Identify the pictures below. Use the word bank below to name each picture.

————————————————

· ·

————————————————

————————————————

· ·

————————————————

Word Bank:

hat	glasses	trunks	deck chair

SUMMER VOCABULARY

Identify the pictures below. Use the word bank below to name each picture.

_____

....

_____

_____

....

_____

_____

....

_____

_____

....

_____

Word Bank:

| ball | Sun | Umbrella | Watermelon |

SUMMER VOCABULARY

Identify the pictures below. Use the word bank below to name each picture.

——————————
....

——————————

——————————
....

——————————

——————————
....

——————————

——————————
....

——————————

Word Bank:

Popsicle	Sandcastle	Crab	sea shells

SUMMER VOCABULARY

Identify the pictures below. Use the word bank below to name each picture.

....

....

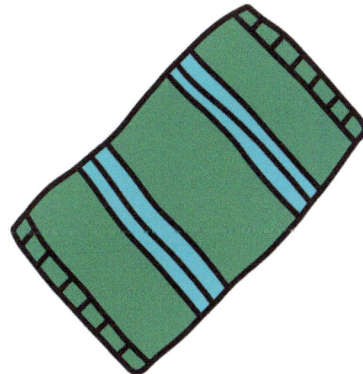

....

....

Word Bank:

Floater	Lounger	Sandbucket	Beach Towel

SENTENCE WRITING

Look at the picture below. Write a sentence that tells about the picture.

_____

....

_____

_____

....

_____

_____

....

_____

SENTENCE WRITING

Look at the picture below. Write a sentence that tells about the picture.

....

_____

....

_____

....

_____

SENTENCE WRITING

Look at the picture below. Write a sentence that tells about the picture.

_____

. . . .

_____

. . . .

_____

. . . .

_____

SENTENCE WRITING

Look at the picture below. Write a sentence that tells about the picture.

SENTENCE WRITING

Look at the picture below. Write a sentence that tells about the picture.

_____

···

_____

_____

···

_____

_____

···

_____

SENTENCE WRITING

Look at the picture below. Write a sentence that tells about the picture.

_____

....

_____

....

_____

....

_____

SENTENCE WRITING

Look at the picture below. Write a sentence that tells about the picture.

_____

....

_____

....

_____

....

_____

SENTENCE WRITING

Look at the picture below. Write a sentence that tells about the picture.

SENTENCE WRITING

Look at the picture below. Write a sentence that tells about the picture.

_____

....

_____

....

_____

....

_____

SENTENCE WRITING

Look at the picture below. Write a sentence that tells about the picture.

_____

....

_____

....

_____

....

_____

Name _____   Date _____

SUMMER ACTIVITY

What is your favorite Summer activity?

_____

· ·

_____

· ·

_____

· ·

_____

· ·

_____

· ·

_____

· ·

_____

_____

· ·

_____

Name _____   Date _____

SUMMER'S BEST THING

What is the best thing about Summer?

_____

....

_____

_____

....

_____

_____

....

_____

_____

....

_____

_____

....

_____

....

_____

_____

....

_____

_____

....

_____

Name _____   Date _____

MY SUMMER FOOD

What is your favorite Summer food and why?

_____

· ·

_____

· ·

_____

· ·

_____

· ·

_____

· ·

_____

· ·

_____

· ·

· ·

_____

· ·

· ·

_____

Name _____   Date _____

MY SUMMER VACATION

What was your favorite thing over the summer break?

_____

....

_____

_____

....

_____

_____

....

_____

_____

....

_____

_____

....

_____

_____

....

_____

....

_____

_____

....

_____

....

_____

Name _____   Date _____

MY FAVORITE ICECREAM

Describe your favorite Ice cream

SUMMER COUNTING

Find and count the following items.

SUMMER GRAPH

Find and graph the items listed. Then answer the questions below.

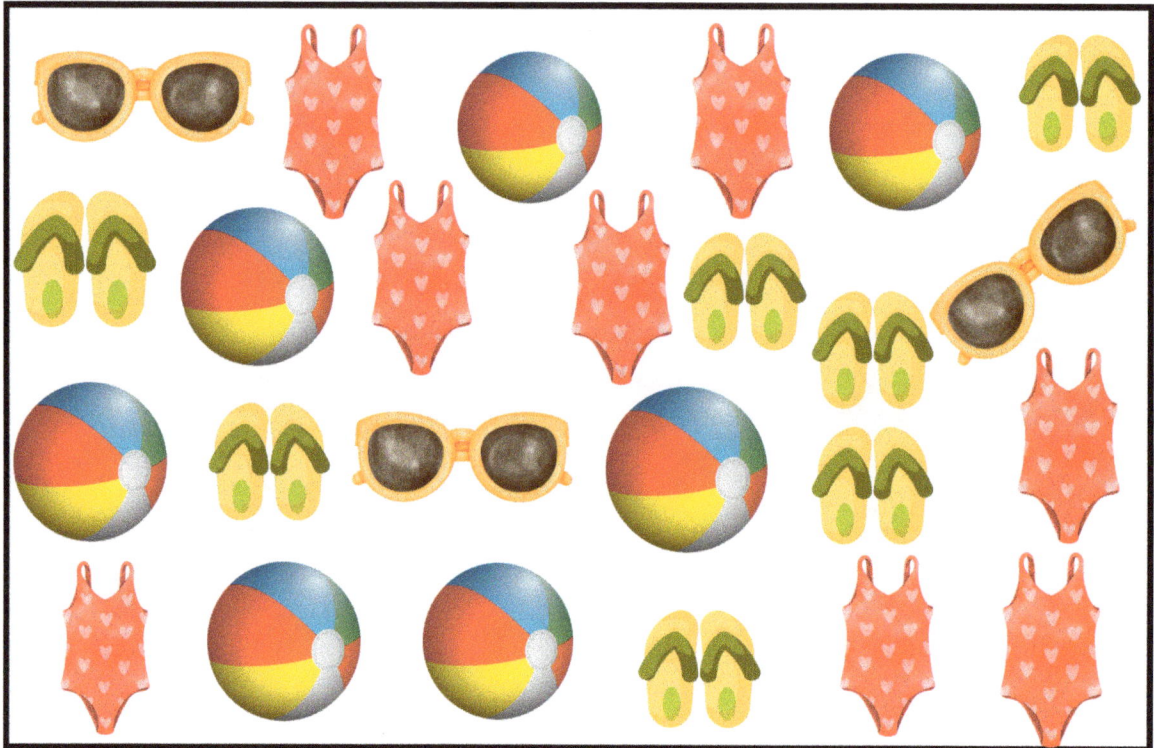

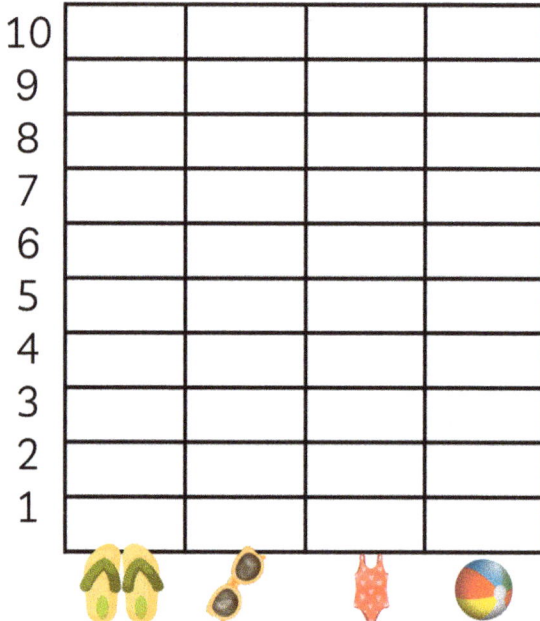

10				
9				
8				
7				
6				
5				
4				
3				
2				
1				

How many of each?

Which item did you find the most of? _____

Which item did you find the least of? _____

SUMMER PATTERNS

Look at the patterns below. Cut out the images at the bottom. Paste the image that comes next in each pattern.

SUMMER PATTERN

Look at the patterns below. Cut out the images at the bottom. Paste the image that comes next in each pattern.

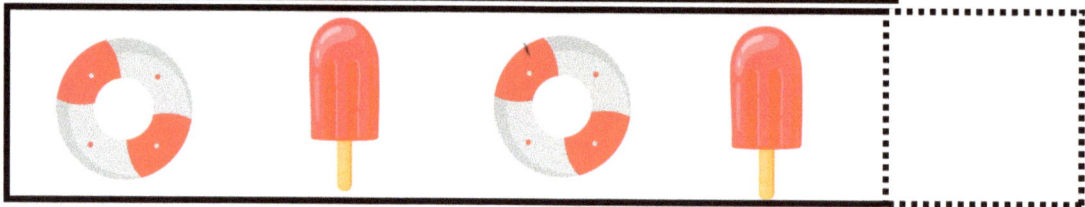

SUMMER PATTERN

Look at the patterns below. Cut out the images at the bottom. Paste the image that comes next in each pattern.

Name _____ Date _____

SUMMER COLORING

Color the picture below.

SUMMER COLORING

Color the picture below.

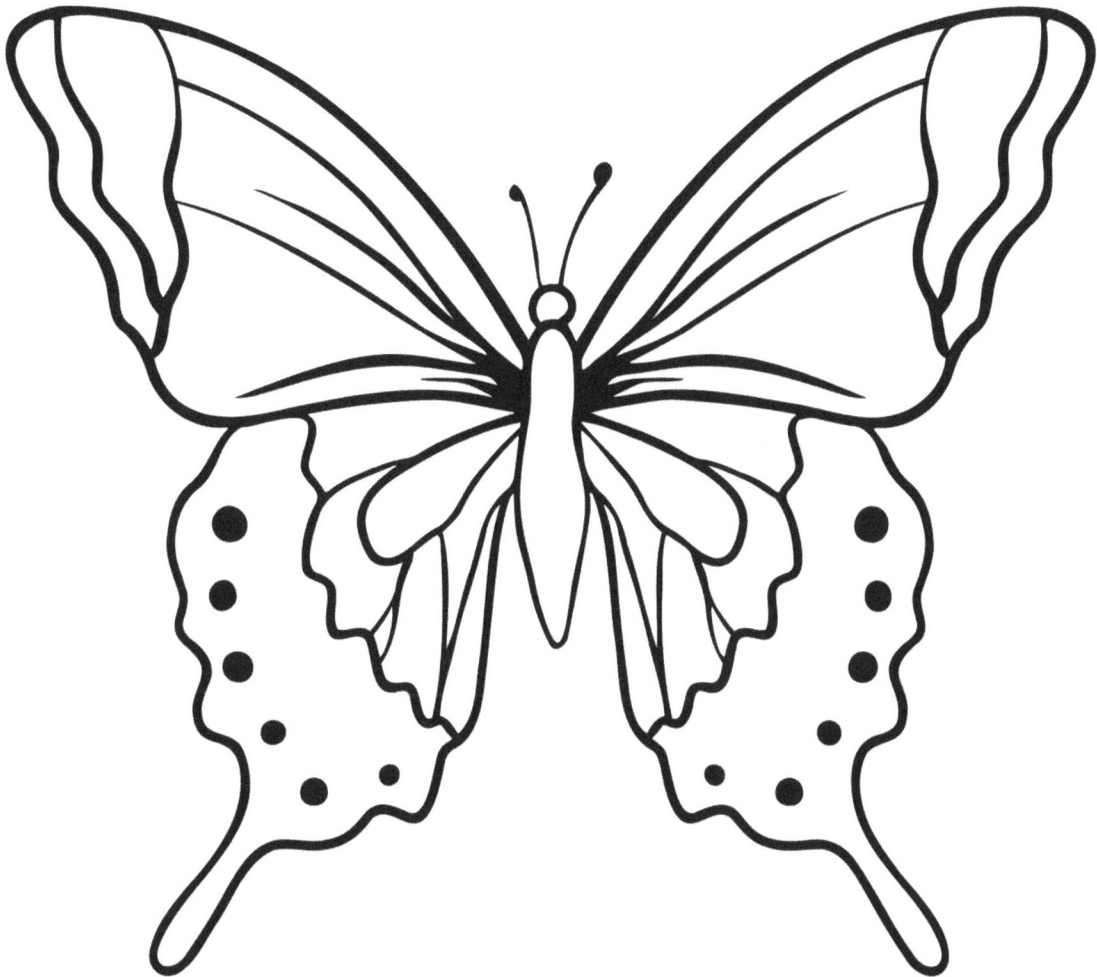

SUMMER COLORING

Color the picture below.

Name _____   Date _____

SUMMER COLORING

Color the picture below.

SUMMER COLORING

Color the picture below.

Name _____   Date _____

SUMMER COLORING

Color the picture below.

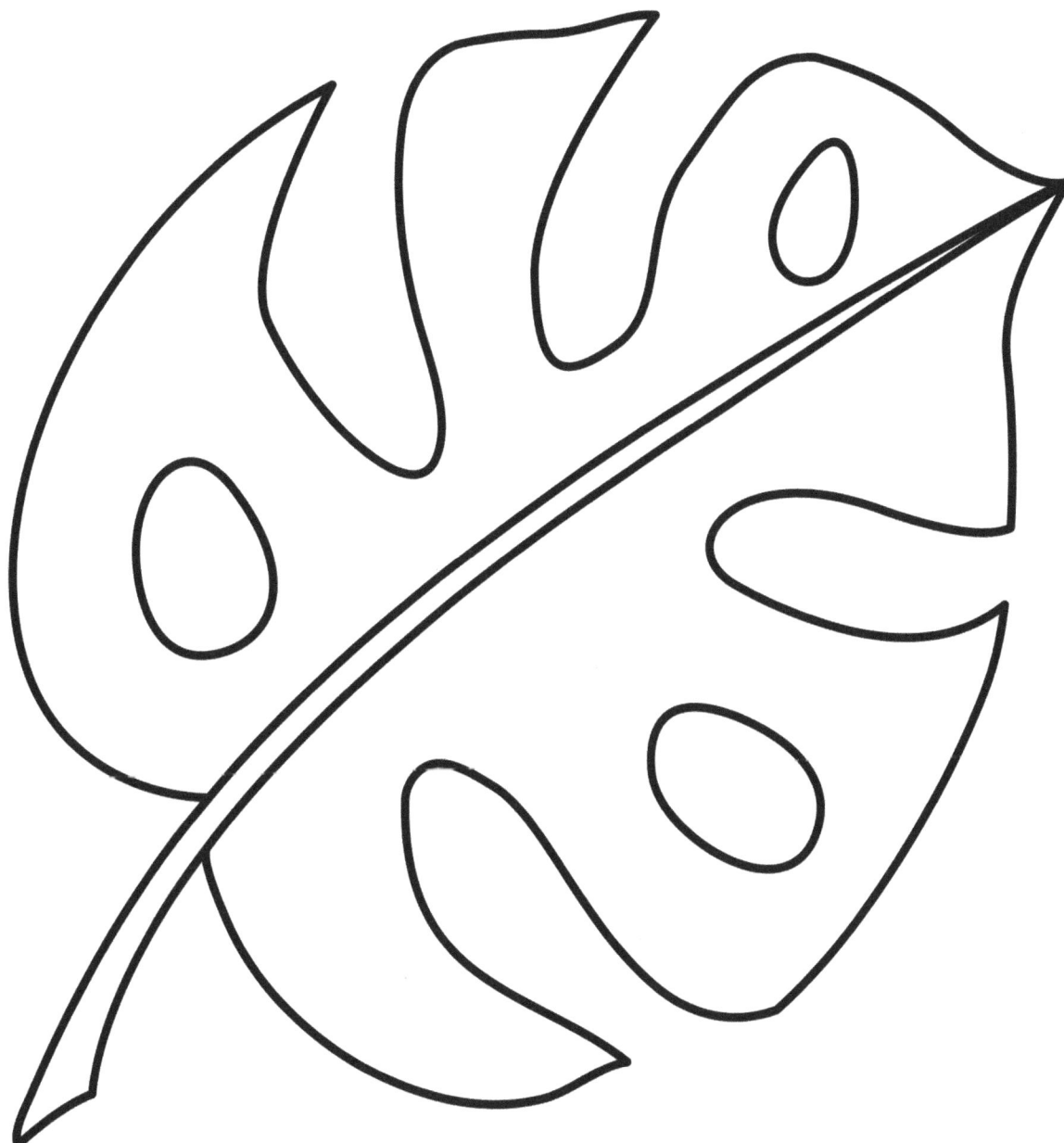

Name _____   Date _____

SUMMER COLORING

Color the picture below.

SUMMER COLORING

Color the picture below.

SUMMER COLORING

Color the picture below.

SUMMER COLORING

Color the picture below.

Check out my other books by Scanning the QR code or using the link below

linktr.ee/beautyinbooks3